A Note to Parents and Teachers

DK READERS is a compelling reading programme for children. The programme is designed in conjunction with leading literacy experts, including Cliff Moon M.Ed., who has spent many years as a teacher and teacher educator specializing in reading. Cliff Moon has written more than 160 books for children and teachers. He is series editor to Collins Big Cat.

Beautiful illustrations and superb full-colour photographs combine with engaging, easy-to-read stories to offer a fresh approach to each subject in the series. Each DK READER is guaranteed to capture a child's interest while developing his or her reading skills, general knowledge, and love of reading.

The five levels of DK READERS are aimed at different reading abilities, enabling you to choose the books that are exactly right for your child:

Pre-level 1: Learning to read
Level 1: Beginning to read
Level 2: Beginning to read alone
Level 3: Reading alone
Level 4: Proficient readers

The "correct" age at which a child begins to read can be anywhere from three to eight years old. Adult participation through the early levels is very helpful for providing encouragement, discussing storylines and sounding out unfamiliar words.

No matter which level you select, you can be sure that you are helping your child learn to read, then read to learn!

LONDON, NEW YORK, MUNICH,
MELBOURNE, AND DELHI

Project Editors Naia Bray-Moffatt
Art Editor Rebecca Johns
Series Editor Deborah Lock
Production Siu Chan
Picture Researcher Sarah Pownall
Illustrator Peter Dennis
Jacket Designer Natalie Godwin
Publishing Manager Bridget Giles

Consultants Dr. Joshua Smith
and Matt Lamanna, and thanks
also to Jason Poole

Reading Consultant
Cliff Moon, M.Ed.

Published in Great Britain by
Dorling Kindersley Limited
80 Strand, London WC2R 0RL

Copyright © 2003 Dorling Kindersley Limited
A Penguin Company
This edition, 2009

2 4 6 8 10 9 7 5 3 1
DD506 – 07/09

A CIP catalogue record for this book
is available from the British Library

ISBN: 978-1-40534-108-0

Colour reproduction by Colourscan, Singapore
Printed and bound in China by L. Rex Printing Co. Ltd.

The publisher would like to thank the following
for their kind permission to reproduce their photographs:
a=above; c=centre; b=below; l=left; r=right t=top;
Bruce Coleman Ltd: 13cl. **Corbis:** Yann Arthus-Bertrand 44bl; Steve Bein
13tr; Annie Griffiths-Belt 13br; Gary Braasch 6 (background); Dave G.
Houser 44t; Photopress Washington/Sygma 8t; Photowodd Inc 4-5; Galen
Rowell 45; Kevin Schafer 5br; Hubert Stradler 12cl; Vo Tung Dung/ Sygma
41tr; Gordon Whitten 12tl. **Roger de la Harpe:** 35b. **Patricia Kane-Vanni:**
14t, 16-17, 17cr, 21tr, 33t, 35c. **Dr. Kenneth Lacovara:** 15b. **Matt
Lamanna:** 18-19, 41bc. **Jerry Harris:** 10t. **Mandela A Lyon:** 35t. **The
Natural History Museum, London:** 38bl. **Nature Picture Library:** Grant
McDowell 22-23. **Tosh Odano:** Courtesy of Dinodon, Inc 47br. **PA Photos:**
46t. **Paleontology Museum, Munich:** 8bl. **Silva Sweden AB:** 5tr. **Dr.
Joshua Smith:** 15t, 28b, 33b. **Allison Tumarkin-Deratzian:** 4bl, 11, 20t,
21b, 26b, 27t, 29tl, 32cl, 32b, 34t, 36-37, 37cr, 39, 49br.
Front jacket: PA Photos.
All other images © Dorling Kindersley
For further information see: www.dkimages.com

Discover more at
www.dk.com

Contents

THE BIG DINOSAUR DIG

Written by Esther Ripley

A Dorling Kindersley Book

Lost and found

Josh Smith climbed out of the 4x4 and gazed across the sand and rocks. Somewhere in this desert he was hoping to find a treasure trove of dinosaur fossils.

In the early 1900s, a fossil hunter had found the bones of huge dinosaurs in part of the Sahara Desert in Egypt. Although this fossil hunter died many years ago, Josh had the map references for one of the dinosaur sites.

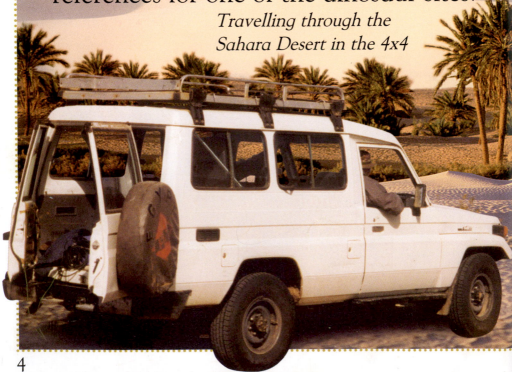

Travelling through the Sahara Desert in the 4x4

They were recorded in his Global Positioning System, or GPS – a handy little computer that uses satellites to help people navigate.

The GPS bleeped repeatedly. It was telling Josh that he had reached the right spot.

But Josh was puzzled. "This doesn't look like it at all," he said to his partner Jen, who was driving. "There's supposed to be a mountain here."

Global Positioning System

Dinosaur fossils

Over millions of years, dinosaur bones buried under layers of rock turn into solid stone, forming fossils.

When Josh was six years old and growing up in Orange, Massachusetts, U.S.A., he was given his first book about dinosaurs. His favourite dinosaur was *Spinosaurus* – a carnivore with a huge fin on its back that stood up like a sail.

The fossilized bones of *Spinosaurus* were discovered in the Bahariya Oasis in the Sahara Desert by a German fossil hunter called Ernst Stromer. Travelling by camel, Stromer made a trip into the desert to dig out the fossilized bones and take them back to Germany.

The skull and teeth of Carcharodontosaurus

Ernst Stromer also unearthed sharp, jagged teeth belonging to another huge meat eater, which he named *Carcharodontosaurus*. There were

Ernst Stromer

also giant, solid bones from a heavyweight sauropod – a plant-eating dinosaur with a long neck and legs like tree trunks. He called it *Aegyptosaurus*, which means "Egyptian lizard".

After years of preparation, an incomplete 15.2 metre-(50-ft-) long skeleton of *Spinosaurus* was put on display in a museum in Munich.

But in 1944, during an air raid on Munich in World War II, a bomb fell on the museum. The building and Stromer's precious dinosaur bones were destroyed.

The skeleton of Spinosaurus, *which means "thorn lizard"*

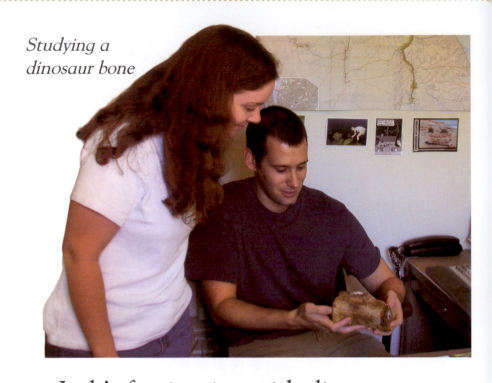

Studying a dinosaur bone

Josh's fascination with dinosaurs continued as he grew up. He went to the University of Pennsylvania to study palaeontology, which is the science of studying life on Earth as it was millions of years ago. For his final degree, Josh had to complete a major project and choose a site for a dig. Josh knew exactly where he wanted to go.

He wanted to follow Stromer's footsteps into the Bahariya Oasis in the Sahara and find more examples of the dinosaur bones that were destroyed in the air raid during the war. If he was really lucky he might even find a new dinosaur.

Removing a dinosaur bone from rock at the University of Pennsylvania

Rocky badlands
of North America

NORTH
AMERICA

EUROPE

*Stromer's site
in Egypt*

PACIFIC
OCEAN

AFRIC

SOUTH
AMERICA

ATLANTIC
OCEAN

Plains and grasslands
in South America

ANTARCTICA

For 180 million years, dinosaurs roamed every part of the earth. Fossil hunters find their bones on every continent – on the plains and grasslands in South America, in the rocky badlands of North America, in quarries in Europe, in the desert in Asia, in Australia and even in the frozen Antarctic.

Desert of Asia

ASIA

INDIAN OCEAN

AUSTRALIA

Antarctica

But for many years, no one had returned to where Stromer had excavated in Africa. This was where Josh and his partner Jen travelled to find out if there were more dinosaur remains.

New dinosaurs

At least seven new types of dinosaur are discovered every year, revealing more and more about life when dinosaurs ruled the world.

Checking the map references

Josh and Jen used Stromer's notes about his expeditions to search for his dinosaur site. But Josh decided that the map reference recorded in his GPS must be wrong. The site was supposed to be at the base of a distinctive cone-shaped mountain called Gebel el Dist, but this was nowhere in sight.

Back in the 4x4, Jen drove east with Josh leaning out of the window, scanning the horizon for Gebel el Dist.

Suddenly he saw something. It looked like a log lying on the sand.

"Can you pull up here, Jen? I need to take a look."

Carefully brushing away the sand, Josh uncovered a thick bone about 30 cm (12 ins) long, broken in three places. He could hardly believe his luck. From its size and shape, Josh guessed it belonged to a large plant eater – perhaps an *Aegyptosaurus*.

Brushing away the sand

Part of the bone that was uncovered

The discovery of one bone was not a big enough find to launch a fossil hunting expedition, but, later that day, Josh and Jen were lucky again. Driving back across the desert, they found Gebel el Dist. The area was littered with pieces of fossilized bone. Josh was very excited. If he could bring a team to Egypt, who knows what they might find.

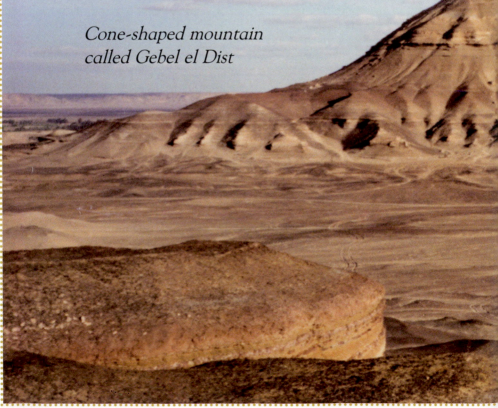

*Cone-shaped mountain
called Gebel el Dist*

Back at home Josh paired up with a palaeontologist friend, Matt Lamanna, to raise the £40,000 they needed for an expedition. They had a good story to tell about Stromer, the dinosaur bones destroyed in the war, and Josh's finds in the desert. A film company decided to sponsor the trip and make a film about it called *The Lost Dinosaurs of Egypt.*

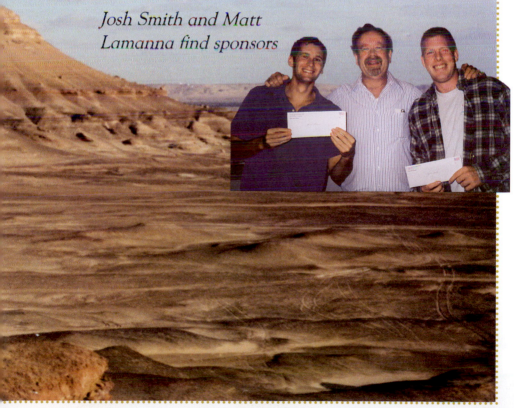

Josh Smith and Matt Lamanna find sponsors

The expedition

Almost a year later, a dig team of palaeontologists and field workers and a film crew rolled into Bawiti, a small mining village in the Bahariya Oasis. Josh, Jen and Matt were also joined by Jason, nicknamed "Chewie" because he reminded everyone of Chewbacca from the *Star Wars* film. Chewie was an expert in preserving fossils.

Fossil hunters usually work in remote places with few comforts, so the team members were surprised and pleased to discover that their lodgings had hot showers and flush toilets.

"We're used to mud huts with a dirt floor and a pit for a toilet," said a delighted Jen.

Bawiti village

The team starts digging at Stromer's old bone pits

The team had only six weeks to find fossilized bones of dinosaurs. Most people think of deserts as hot places, but in winter it can get very cold. Digging hard kept the team warm during the day, but as soon as the sun went down, it was freezing.

After two weeks of digging, they had had little success. There were plenty of small pieces of fossils on the surface of the sand, but when they dug down, there was nothing underneath. Everyone was disappointed.

Small pieces of fossils

Chewie took a break from excavating
a shallow pit and studied the horizon.
"A sandstorm's coming," he shouted.

Within half an hour a biting wind
swept in, sending stinging sand into
the diggers' eyes, noses and mouths.
Josh lay flat on his stomach with his
bandanna tied over his face trying
to brush sand from what might be
a bone embedded in some rock.

"This is pretty stupid," he said. "I'm uncovering something and 30 seconds later it's covered up again. But it's only a small scrap of bone anyway."

Josh was worried that the bones might have crumbled away to dust.

"Maybe this is all there is," he wondered. "Perhaps Stromer discovered everything, and there is nothing left for us to find."

Protective gear
It's important to wear proper clothing on a dig. Gloves protect hands from jagged rocks, and goggles keep eyes free of stinging sand.

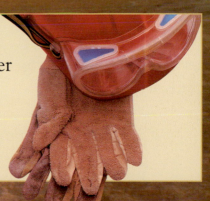

Deeply buried dinosaur skeletons
are brought closer to the earth's surface
when earthquakes disturb the rock layers.

*1. A whole dinosaur
skeleton before it
becomes buried
deep in the earth.*

*2. Minerals and
water in the rock
turn the bones to
stone over time.*

*3. Movements in the earth
gradually push the skeleton
towards the surface.*

Fossil hunters
find the remains
in canyons and cliffs
where many layers of rock
are exposed, or on ground
shifted by landslides. Then
they use hammers, pickaxes and drills
to get to them. Often the weather does
the hard work and the bones end up
close to the surface. In the desert, wind
and sandstorms wear away the layers
of rock. But if no one finds the bones,
they crumble away to dust.

Pickaxe

Chisel

Hammer

*4. Fossil hunters
discover the bones.*

The big bone

Josh began to think about the broken bone he had found with Jen on their first trip a year earlier. It was right on the surface and there was probably not much underneath it. But why not take the team back there to look?

Throwing their tools into the 4x4s, the fossil hunters, together with the film crew, headed off to the new site.

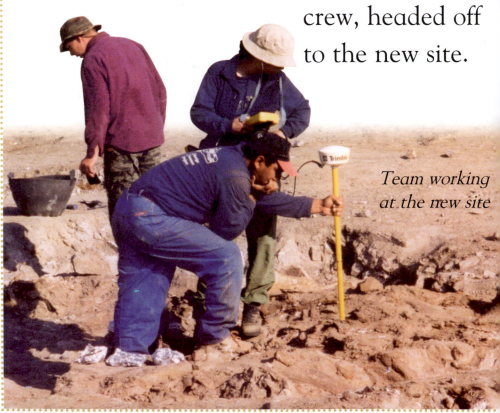

Team working at the new site

Dinosaur fossils uncovered

The bone was lying just as Josh had left it. Not far away the team could see more bones. Grabbing shovels and hammers, the workers began to pick away at the soft rock beneath the sand. Almost immediately they found what they had been searching for – glimpses of large bones embedded in the rock. They had struck dinosaur gold.

The bone quarry buzzed with excitement. Josh was chipping along the edge of a large bone using a dental pick and brushes. A few feet away Chewie was chiseling out something just as big. Then they realized they were working on two sides of the same bone.

"This is the top end of a humerus," Chewie cried, identifying the curved upper-arm bone.

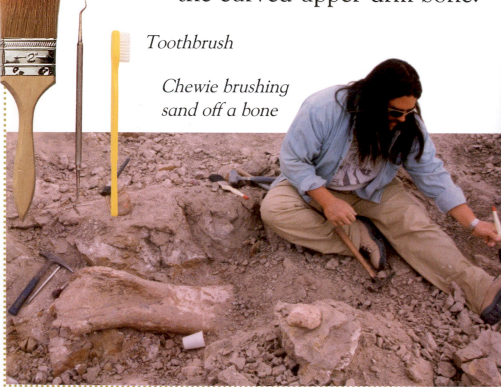

Paint brush

Dental pick

Toothbrush

Chewie brushing sand off a bone

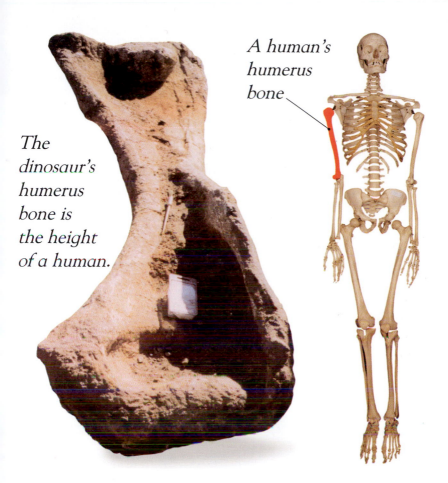

The dinosaur's humerus bone is the height of a human.

A human's humerus bone

"Can't be," laughed Josh. "If this is the top, the other end will be way down there. Nothing's got a humerus that big."

After a day of hard digging, Josh and Chewie presented the biggest humerus they had ever seen. It was 1.7 metres (5 ft 7ins) long – as tall as a man.

The humerus belonged
to a sauropod – a long-necked
plant-eating dinosaur – that
roamed in the Cretaceous Period.
The size of its bones told Josh that
the sauropod he had found was very big.

It normally takes months to dig up
the bones of such a large dinosaur,
but the team had just three weeks left.

Aegyptosaurus

Spinosaurus

Dinosaur times
The earliest dinosaurs lived
230 million years ago. The
last ones died out at the end
of the Cretaceous Period,
about 65 million years ago.

TRIASSIC PERIOD
230–208 million years ago

JURASSIC PERIOD
208–145 million years ago

The huge sauropod

Carcharodontosaurus

CRETACEOUS PERIOD
145–65 million years ago

31

The diggers hacked out a large block of sandstone containing a fossil by digging a trench around it leaving a column of earth underneath.

Then they painted the bone with a special glue to prevent it from crumbling, and covered it with aluminum foil for protection.

Putting on the plaster of Paris is just like wrapping a broken arm in a cast.

Next they put on a jacket of bandages and plaster of Paris to protect the bone while they freed it from its column and dragged it slowly out of the pit.

Chewie drew diagrams to show exactly where the bones were lying to help them fit the bones together later.

The sketch shows the position where the bones were discovered.

E

N

Scapula

Right humerus

Vertebrae

2 m (6.5 ft)

Scapula

Shed theropod tooth crown

Left humerus

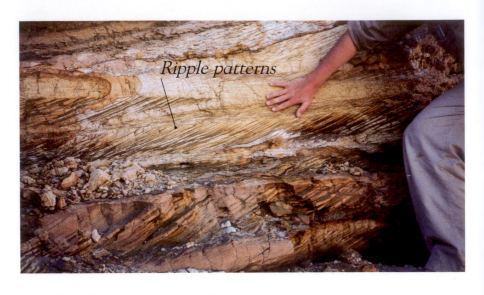

Ripple patterns

Mud rocks showing ripples

The team also found patterns of ripples and waves on what was once deep mud, as well as fossils of ferns and roots. This meant their sauropod was not standing on dry sand – it was walking in a seaside swamp full of lush plant life.

Shifting Earth
The surface of Earth shifts constantly. During the age of the dinosaurs, continents collided and broke apart and oceans came and went.

Matt found another site littered with the fossils of fish, turtles, crocodiles and other creatures that lived in this tidal mudflat.

Leaf fossil

This was more evidence that the dusty desert may have been a very different place 100 million years ago.

Fossilized skull bone of a giant coelacanth *fish*

As the days sped by, the pile of rocks and fossilized bones grew. The field workers had shifted five and a half tons. In their plaster jackets, some of the fossils weighed as much as a steel girder. The team winched the heavy ones onto a flatbed truck. On the last night they worked by moonlight. Then the bones had to be shipped back to the U.S.A.

Once there, the bones and fossils could be examined in the university's laboratories. Josh and his team had dug up a giant. But they would need to do a great deal of research before they knew exactly what kind of giant they had found.

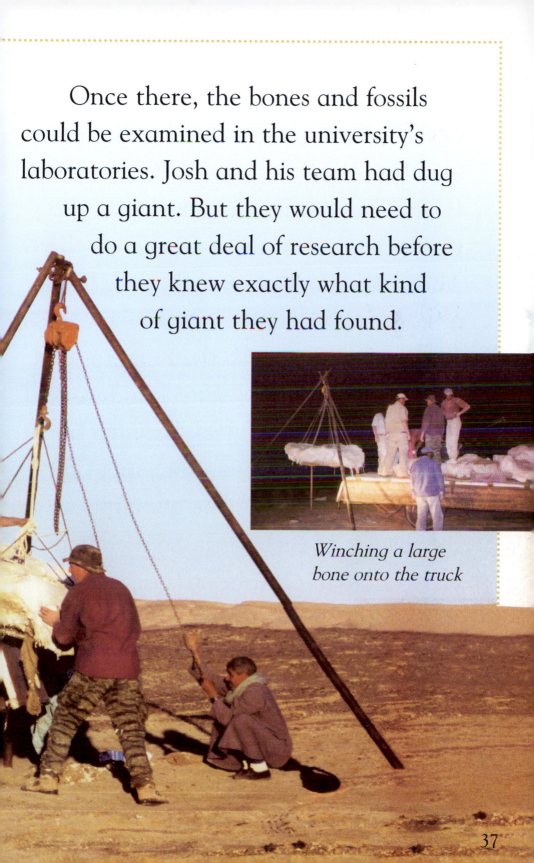

Winching a large bone onto the truck

The tidal giant

In the laboratory, Chewie and his team of palaeo-detectives had delicate work to do. They used a cast saw to cut the plaster jackets off the bones. Then the painstaking task of removing the fossils from the rock began.

Chewie began with the humerus and some vertebrae (backbones) and worked with an airscribe – a jack hammer about the size of a marker pen that taps off tiny pieces of rock. As he got closer to the surface of each fossil, he used dental picks and paint brushes to brush away dust. As soon as the fossil was exposed, he painted it with a liquid plastic to prevent it from breaking.

Using an airscribe to remove rock

Palaeo-detectives carefully remove the fossil from the rock.

It took almost a year to process the fossils. In the end, there were enough bones to build about a quarter of a dinosaur but not enough for a complete skeleton. However, by comparing the bones with similar dinosaurs, the team could figure out what their creature would have been like.

The dinosaur was about ten times heavier than an elephant.

Only one bone, as long as Chewie's forearm, didn't seem to fit anywhere – until Chewie realized it was a huge toe!

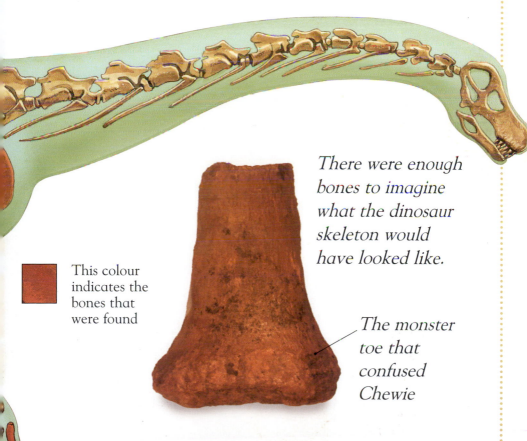

There were enough bones to imagine what the dinosaur skeleton would have looked like.

This colour indicates the bones that were found

The monster toe that confused Chewie

Although there were not enough bones to reconstruct their dinosaur, the team knew enough about sauropods to make some good guesses about its appearance. They could see where muscles were once attached to bones. This helped them flesh out their dinosaur.

They imagined the creature would have moved through the swamp with the lumbering movements of an elephant.

No one knows what colour dinosaurs were, so Josh could choose whatever colour he liked.

"Let's make ours green," he said.

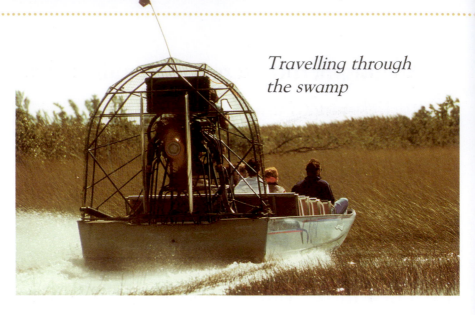

Travelling through the swamp

Josh and the team geologist, Ken Lacovara, wanted to find out more about the environment in which their seashore giant lived, so they travelled into the biggest swamp in the U.S.A – the Everglades in Florida. The region is peppered with

many thousands of tiny islands. Tides from the Gulf of Mexico lap over the mud.

Alligators, manatees, fish and turtles swam beneath the water, but Josh and Ken were more interested in tree roots and deposits of mud and sand. These matched what they had found in the desert. Now they felt sure that their dinosaur had lived in a tropical swamp.

Alligators swimming between tree roots

A year and a half after their dig in the desert, Josh announced the team's discovery to the press. Their sauropod was huge. It was about 25 metres (80 ft) long and weighed up to 50 tons.

It would fill a tennis court easily. It was one of the biggest dinosaurs ever found. More importantly, its bones were slightly different from anything that had been found before. They had discovered a new species of dinosaur.

If you find a new dinosaur, you get to name it. The team chose *Paralititan stromeri*. *Paralititan* is Greek for "tidal giant", which suits a creature that lived in a tidal swamp. *Stromeri* is a tribute to Stromer, the palaeontologist who started Josh and his friends on the path to their adventures.

Heavyweight champion
The heaviest dinosaur is a plant eater from South America. *Argentinosaurus* is believed to weigh around 100 tons.

The vertebrae of Argentinosaurus

Glossary

Badlands
A bleak landscape where great expanses of rock are exposed to the weather.

Bandanna
A colourful cotton scarf.

Cast saw
A saw that is used to cut away a plaster cast from a fossil.

Cretaceous Period
Part of Earth's history that lasted from 145 million years ago until the dinosaurs died out 65 million years ago.

Dinosaurs
Land reptiles that lived between 230 to 65 million years ago. The name dinosaur is the Greek word for "terrible lizard".

Earthquakes
Tremors and shaking of the earth's surface, which usually occurs along faults (fractures or breaks) in the earth's layers.

Everglades
A huge area of swamp with thousands of tiny islands in Florida on the Gulf of Mexico in the U.S.A.

Fossils
Traces of animals and plants that have been preserved in rocks.

Humerus
A bone of the upper arm in a human or the upper front leg in a four-legged animal.

Jurassic Period
The middle period of the age of the dinosaurs that lasted from 208 to 145 million years ago.

Manatee
A rare plant-eating mammal that lives in water, and is in danger of becoming extinct.

Palaeontology
The science of life on Earth as it was millions of years ago.

Sahara Desert
The largest desert in the world covering a huge area of North Africa.

Sauropod
One of a group of plant-eating dinosaurs with long necks and legs like tree trunks.

Spinosaurus
A long, slender meat-eating dinosaur about 15.2 metres (50 ft) long with a huge fin on its back.

Triassic period
Part of Earth's history that lasted from 230 to 208 million years ago during which the dinosaurs first appeared.

Pronunciation Guide
Carcharodontosaurus
Kahr-KAR-o-DON-to-SAWR-us
Bahariya
Ba-har-EE-uh
Aegyptosaurus
Ee-JIP-tuh-SAWR-us
Paralititan
Pah-RAL-i-TI-tan